solzhenitsyn

A PICTORIAL AUTOBIOGRAPHY

FARRAR, STRAUS AND GIROUX
NEW YORK

Printed in the United States of America

Published simultaneously in Canada by Doubleday Canada Ltd., Toronto

First printing, 1974

Library of Congress Cataloging in Publication Data.

Solzhenitsyn, Aleksandr Isaevich.
    Solzhenitsyn: a pictorial autobiography.

    Translation of a French collection entitled Soljénitsyne; includes complete text of the author's brief autobiography written for the Nobel Committee, and excerpts from his other writings.
    1. Solzhenitsyn, Aleksandr Isaevich.
I. Title.
PG3488.04A24   1974   891.7'8'4409 [B]   74-7070

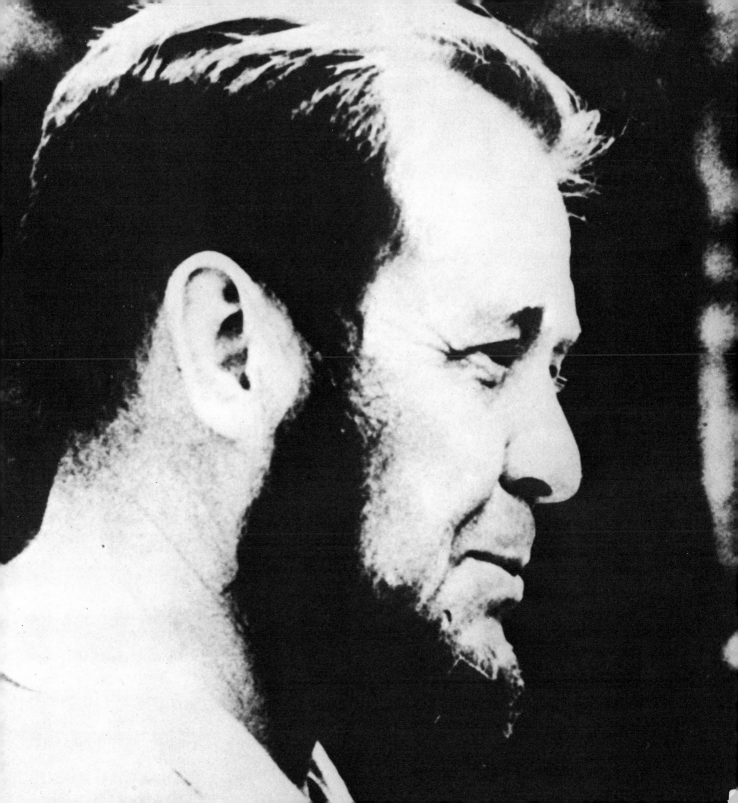

solzhenitsyn

The sight of a man saying no with his bare hands is one of the things that most mysteriously and profoundly stir the hearts of men.

André Malraux

What surprises me most in Solzhenitsyn is the calm that he emanates—he who has been threatened and fought over more than any other man on earth. Nothing, it seems, can destroy his serenity, neither the terrible insults to which he has been exposed in his own country nor the banishment—the "one-way ticket"—which he has been offered and which he has refused. At the same time, Solzhenitsyn's calm is not at all that of a gilded Olympian monument but that of a living man, concerned and involved with the course of human events.

Heinrich Böll

I was born on December 11, 1918, in Kislovodsk. My father, a student in the philology department of Moscow University, did not complete the required program because he volunteered for the army in 1914. He became an artillery officer on the German front, served through the entire war, and died in the summer of 1918, half a year before I was born. I was brought up by my mother, a typist and stenographer, in Rostov-on-Don, where I spent my childhood and my teens. I finished high school there in 1936.

From the time I was very young I had had, on my own, a longing to become a writer and had written much of the usual youthful nonsense and, in the thirties, had made attempts to get published, but my manuscripts were not accepted anywhere. I had in mind getting a literary education, but Rostov did not offer what I wanted; to go to Moscow was impossible because of my mother's being single and ill and our very modest means.

My mother raised me in very
difficult conditions. She was widowed
before I was born and never remarried, mainly
because she was afraid that a stepfather would be too
strict. We lived in Rostov for nineteen years before
the war, and for fifteen of those we could not get
a room from the state. All the time we had to find some
broken-down little hut which we could rent from private
owners for a great deal of money. And when we finally
did get a room, it was part of a reconstructed stable.
It was always cold. There was a draft. The
coal we used for heat was hard to get. Water had to be
carried from afar. I actually only learned recently
what running water in an apartment meant.
Mama knew French and English well, and
had also studied shorthand and typing, but agencies
that paid well never hired her, because of her
social origin.

My only memory of my father is from photographs
and the stories told by my mother and other people
who knew him. While a student at the university he
volunteered for the army, and he served in the
Grenadier Artillery Brigade. Once when the battery
was set afire, he saved some munitions boxes himself.
The three officer's decorations that he left from
World War I—which in my childhood were considered
the mark of a dangerous criminal—were buried by
my mother and me out of fear of a search.
When the whole front was collapsing,
my father's battery remained on the front lines until
the Treaty of Brest. My mother and father were married
at the front by a brigade priest.
Papa returned home in the spring of
1918, and soon thereafter died as a result of an accident
and poor medical care. His grave in Georgievsk was
leveled by a tractor in the construction of a stadium.

Therefore I enrolled in the mathematics department of Rostov University; I had considerable aptitude for mathematics, I could do it easily, but it never appealed to me as a life's work. However, it served as a benefactor in my destiny. At least twice it saved my life: probably I would not have survived eight years of the camps if, as a mathematician, I had not been assigned for four years to a so-called sharashka; and in exile I was allowed to teach mathematics and physics, which made life easier and gave me a chance to get down to the job of writing. If I had had a literary education, I doubt I would have come through my ordeals intact; I would have been under a great handicap.

To be sure, I did begin literary studies later: from 1939 to 1941, along with the physics and math, I was a student in the correspondence department of Moscow's Institute of History, Philosophy, and Literature.

In 1941, a few days before the beginning of the war, I graduated from the physics and math program of Rostov University. With the war's outbreak, I, because of restrictions due to health, became driver of a wagon train and with it spent the winter of 1941-2. Only later—again thanks to mathematics—was I transferred to artillery school, where I completed the accelerated course by November 1942.

At that time I was appointed commander of a reconnaissance artillery battery and uninterruptedly held that position during my military service, never leaving the front, until my arrest in February 1945. That occurred in East Prussia, a place strangely connected with my destiny: as far back as 1937, while still a first-year university student, I selected as a topic the "Samsonov Catastrophe" of 1914 in East Prussia, studied all the books about it, and in 1945 with my own two feet walked the very same ground. (Now, in the fall of 1970, the book that deals with it, "August 1914," is finished.)

I was arrested on the basis of censored extracts from my correspondence with a school friend in 1944-5, basically for disrespectful remarks about Stalin, although we referred to him by a pseudonym. Material complementing the "accusation" was rough drafts of stories and reflections found in my map case. Nevertheless, this was not sufficient for a "trial," and in June 1945 I was "convicted" by a procedure that was then widespread —in my absence, by a decision of OSO (an NKVD Special Tribunal)—and sentenced to eight years in a labor camp (at that time this was considered a mitigated sentence).

At first I served my sentence in corrective labor camps of the mixed type (described in my play "The Love-Girl and the Innocent").

Mine was, probably, the easiest imaginable kind of arrest. It did not tear me from the embrace of kith and kin, nor wrench me from a deeply cherished home life. One pallid European February it took me from our narrow salient on the Baltic Sea, where, depending on one's point of view, either we had surrounded the Germans or they had surrounded us, and it deprived me only of my familiar artillery battery and the scenes of the last three months of the war.

The brigade commander called me to his headquarters and asked me for my pistol; I turned it over without suspecting any evil intent, when suddenly, from a tense, immobile suite of staff officers in the corner, two counterintelligence officers stepped forward hurriedly, crossed the room in a few quick bounds, their four hands grabbed simultaneously at the star on my cap, my shoulder boards, my officer's belt, my map case, and they shouted theatrically:

"You are under arrest!"

Burning and prickling from head to toe, all I could exclaim was:

"Me? What for?"

And even though there is usually no answer to this question, surprisingly I received one! This is worth recalling, because it is so contrary to our usual custom. Hardly had the SMERSH men finished "plucking" me and taken my notes on

political subjects, along with my map case, and begun to push me as quickly as possible toward the exit, urged on by the German shellfire rattling the windowpanes, than I heard myself firmly addressed — yes! Across the sheer gap separating me from those left behind, the gap created by the heavy-falling word "arrest," across that quarantine line not even a sound dared penetrate, came the unthinkable, magic words of the brigade commander:

"Solzhenitsyn. Come back here."

With a sharp turn I broke away from the hands of the SMERSH men and stepped back to the brigade commander. I had never known him very well. He had never condescended to run-of-the-mill conversations with me. To me his face had always conveyed an order, a command, wrath. But right now it was illuminated in a thoughtful way. Was it from shame for his own involuntary part in this dirty business? Was it from an impulse to rise above the pitiful sub-ordination of a whole lifetime? Ten days before, I had led my own reconnaissance battery almost intact out of the fire pocket in which the twelve heavy guns of his artillery battalion had been left, and now he had to renounce me because of a piece of paper with a seal on it?

"You have …" he asked weightily, "a friend on the

First Ukrainian Front?"

"It's forbidden! You have no right!" the captain and the major of counterintelligence shouted at the colonel. In the corner, the suite of staff officers crowded closer to each other in fright, as if they feared to share the brigade commander's unbelievable rashness (the political officers among them already preparing to present materials against him). But I had already understood: I knew instantly I had been arrested because of my correspondence with a school friend, and understood from what direction to expect danger.

Zakhar Georgiyevich Travkin could have stopped right there! But no! Continuing his attempt to expunge his part in this and to stand erect before his own conscience, he rose from behind his desk—he had never stood up in my presence in my former life—and reached across the quarantine line that separated us and gave me his hand, although he would never have reached out his hand to me had I remained a free man. And pressing my hand, while his whole suite stood there in mute horror, showing that warmth that may appear in an habitually severe face, he said fearlessly and precisely:

"I wish you happiness, Captain!"

Not only was I no longer a captain, but I had been exposed

as an enemy of the people (for among us every person is totally exposed from the moment of arrest). And he had wished happiness—to an enemy?

The panes rattled. The German shells tore up the earth two hundred yards away, reminding one that this could not have happened back in the rear, under the ordinary circumstances of established existence, but only out here, under the breath of death, which was not only close by but in the face of which all were equal.

The Gulag Archipelago

Subsequently, in 1946, as a mathematician, I was pulled out and transferred into the system of MVD-MGB scientific research institutes, and in that sort of "special prison" ("The First Circle") spent the middle period of my sentence. In 1950 I was transferred to the then newly created special camps for political prisoners only. In such a camp in Ekibastuz in Kazakhstan ("One Day in the Life of Ivan Denisovich") I worked as a laborer, bricklayer, and smelter. There I developed a cancerous tumor, operated on but not cured (its nature was recognized only later).

Following a month-long holdover at the end of my eight-year term, there came—without a new sentence and even without a "decree by the OSO"—an administrative decision not to free me but to send me to perpetual exile in Kokterek (southern Kazakhstan).

 His reddish hair was neither thin nor gray, but there were already many deep wrinkles in his drawn face—whole wreaths of them around his eyes, at the corners of his lips, long furrows on his forehead. His skin looked faded because of the lack of fresh air. But it was most of all his economy of movement that made him seem old —that wise economy with which nature husbands a prisoner's strength against the drain of a concentration-camp regime. True, in the relative freedom of the sharashka, where the diet included meat and energy wasn't burned up in physical labor, there was no real need for economy of movement; but Nerzhin understood the uncertain nature of his prison sentence, and practiced that restriction of effort to ensure its becoming a permanent habit.

The First Circle

Shukhov went off to sleep, and he was completely content. Fate had been kind to him in many ways that day: he hadn't been put in the cells, the gang hadn't been sent to the Socialist Community Center, he'd fiddled himself an extra bowl of porridge for dinner, the gang leader had fixed a good percentage, he'd been happy building that wall, he'd slipped through the search with that bit of blade, he'd earned himself something from Tsesar in the evening, he'd bought his tobacco. And he hadn't fallen ill—he had overcome his sickness of the morning.

The day had gone by without a single cloud—almost a happy day.

There were three thousand six hundred and fifty-three days in his sentence, from reveille to lights out.

The three extra days were because of the leap years...

One Day in the Life of Ivan Denisovich

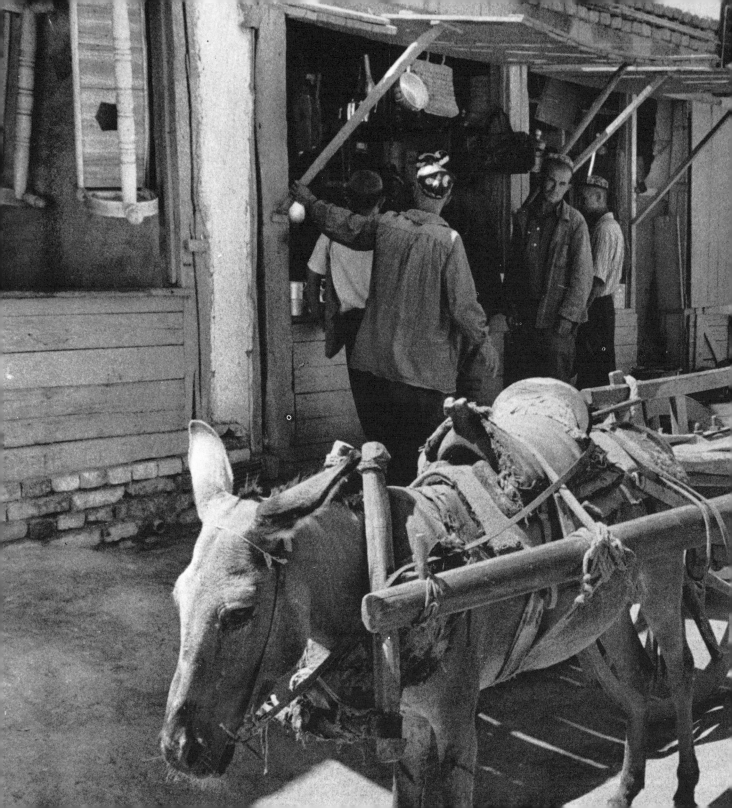

This was not something specially meted out to me but a measure widely used at that time. From March 1953 (on March 5, the day Stalin's death was announced, I was for the first time let out on the street without guards) to June 1956, I served this exile. Here the cancer rapidly developed, and at the end of 1953 I was on the verge of death, unable to eat or sleep and infected by the tumor's poisons. Released to go to Tashkent for treatment, however, during 1954 in the cancer clinic there I was cured ("Cancer Ward," "The Right Hand"). During all the years in exile I taught mathematics and physics in a rural school and, given my austere and solitary way of life, secretly wrote prose (in camp, I could only compose verse by heart). I managed to preserve it and to bring it with me from exile into the European part of the country, where I continued to be outwardly busy teaching, secretly busy writing, at first in Vladimir District ("Matryona's House") and then in Ryazan.

When I arrived in Tashkent that winter I was practically a corpse. I came there expecting to die.

But I was given another lease of life.

A month passed, then another and a third. Outside, the vivid Tashkent spring unfolded and advanced into summer; it was already very warm and lush greenery was everywhere when I started to venture out of doors on my shaky legs.

I still did not dare to admit to myself that I was getting better; in my wildest dreams I still measured my extra span of life not in years but in months. I would tread slowly along the gravel and asphalt paths in the park which was laid out between the blocks of the clinic. I would often have to sit down for a rest and sometimes, when overcome with nausea, I had to lie down with my head as low as possible.

I was like the sick people all around me, and yet I was different: I had fewer rights than they had and was forced to be more silent. People came to visit them, relatives wept for them, and their one concern, their one aim in life was to get well again. But if I recovered, it would be almost pointless: I was thirty-five years of age and yet in that spring I had no one I could call my own in the whole world. I did not even own a passport, and if I were to recover, I should have to leave this green, abundant land and go back to my desert where I had been exiled "in perpetuity." There I was under open surveillance, reported on every fortnight, and for a long time the local police headquarters had not even allowed me, a dying man, to go away for treatment.

I could not talk about all this to the free patients around me; had I done so they would not have understood.

The Right Hand

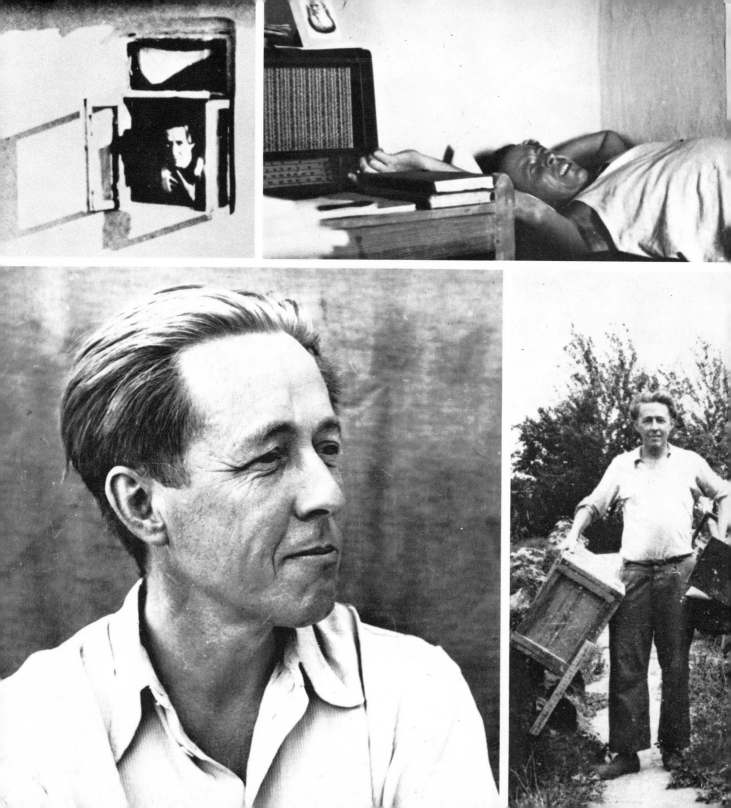

"Ush-Terek" means
"Three Poplars" and is named
after three ancient poplars which are
visible for ten kilometers or more across the
steppe. The trees stand close together, not straight
and slender as most poplars are, but slightly twisted.
They must have been about four hundred years old. Once
they'd reached their present height they'd stopped trying to
grow any higher and branched out sideways, weaving a dense
shadow across the main irrigation channel. It was said that
there had been more of them in the "aul" once, but that they had
been cut down in 1931. Trees like that wouldn't take root these
days. No matter how many the Young Pioneers planted, the goats
picked them to bits as soon as they sprouted. Only American
maple flourished—in the main street in front of the regional
Party committee building.
Which place on earth should you love more? The place
where you crawled out of the womb, a screaming infant,
understanding nothing, not even the evidence of your
eyes or ears? Or the place where they first said to
you, "All right, you can go without a guard
now, you can go—by yourself"?
On your own two legs.
"Take up thy bed and walk!"

Cancer Ward

45

But it was Beetle that Oleg would see in his mind's eye as he strolled along the pathways of the Medical Center, Beetle's huge benevolent head. Not Beetle out in the street but Beetle looming in his window. Suddenly his head would appear, and there he was standing on his hind legs, peering in just like a human being. Tobik was sure to be jumping up and down beside him, and Nikolai Ivanovich would soon be arriving. Deeply moved, Oleg knew now that he was completely content with his lot, quite resigned to his exile. Health was all he asked of the heavens. He wasn't asking for any miracle.

Cancer Ward

By then we had walked as far as a little dammed-up stream crossed by a bridge. There was no prettier spot in the whole village—two or three willows, a crooked little shack, ducks swimming on the pond, and geese waddling up the bank to shake themselves.

"Well, I suppose we'd better try Matryona," said my guide, already growing tired of me. "Only her place isn't that well kept, she's let it go on account of her being so sick."

Matryona's house was nearby. It had a row of four windows along the side on which the sun never shone, a steep shingled roof with an elaborately ornamental dormer window.

Matryona's House

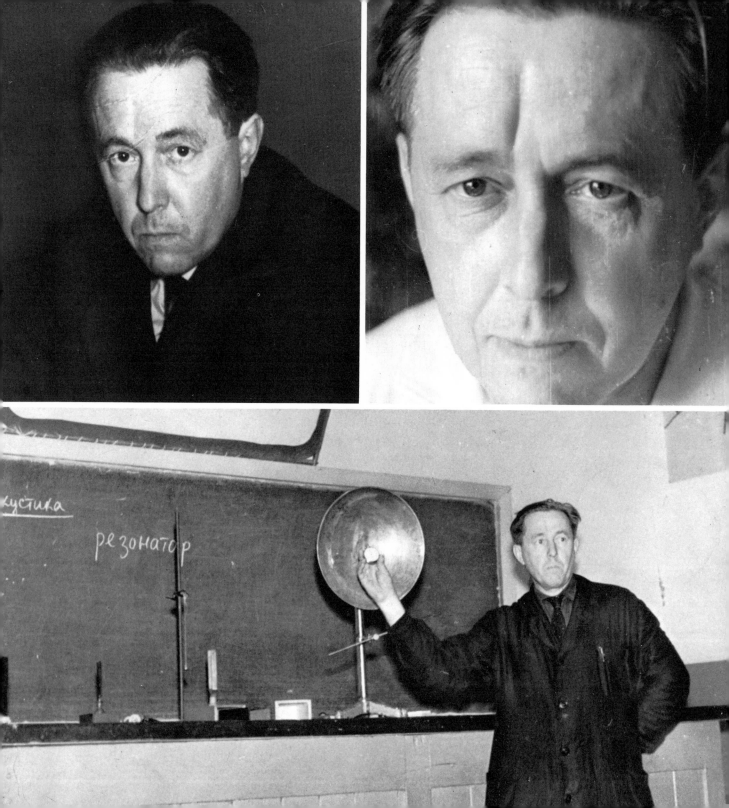

А. СОЛЖЕНИЦЫН

★

ОДИН ДЕНЬ ИВАНА ДЕНИСОВИЧА

Повесть

ВМЕСТО ПРЕДИСЛОВИЯ

Жизненный материал, положенный в основу повести А. Солженицына, необычен в советской литературе. Он несет в себе отзвук тех болезненных явлений в нашем развитии, связанных с периодом развенчанного и отвергнутого партией культа личности, которые по времени хотя и отстоят от нас не так уже далеко, представляются нам далеким прошлым. Но прошлое, каким бы оно ни было, никогда не становится безразличным для настоящего. Залог полного и бесповоротного разрыва со всем тем в прошлом, чем оно было омрачено,— в правдивом и мужественном постижении до конца его последствий. Об этом именно говорил Н. С. Хрущев в своем памятном для всех нас заключительном слове на XXII съезде: «Наш долг тщательно и всесторонне разобраться в такого рода делах, связанных со злоупотреблением властью. Пройдет время, мы умрем, все мы смертны, но, пока работаем, мы можем и должны многое выяснить и сказать правду партии и народу... Это надо сделать для того, чтобы подобные явления впредь никогда не повторялись».

«Один день Ивана Денисовича» — это не документ в мемуарном смысле, не записки или воспоминания о пережитом автором лично, хотя только пережитое лично могло сообщить этому рассказу такую достоверность и подлинность. Это произведение художественное, и в силу именно художнического освещения данного жизненного материала оно является свидетельством особой ценности, документом искусства, возможность которого на этом «специфическом материале» до сих пор представлялась маловероятной.

Читатель не найдет в повести А. Солженицына всеобъемлющего изображения того исторического периода, который, в частности, отмечен горькой памятью тридцать седьмого года. Содержание «Одного дня», естественно, ограничено и временем, и местом действия, и кругозором главного героя повести. Но один день из жизни лагерного заключенного Ивана Денисовича Шухова под пером А. Солженицына, впервые выступающего в литературе, вырастает в картину, наделенную необычайной живостью и верностью правде человеческих характеров. В этом прежде всего заключается редкостная впечатляющая сила произведения. Многих людей, обрисованных здесь в трагическом качестве «зэков», читатель может представить себе и в иной обстановке — на фронте или на стройках послевоенных лет. Это те же люди, волею обстоятельств поставленные в особые, крайние условия жестоких физических и моральных испытаний.

В этой повести нет нарочитого нагнетания ужасных фактов жестокости и произвола, явившихся следствием нарушения советской законности. Автором избран один из самых обычных дней лагерной жизни от подъема до отбоя. Однако этот «обычный» день не может не отозваться в сердце читателя горечью и болью за судьбу людей, которые встают перед ним со страниц повести такими живыми и близкими. Но несомненная победа художника в том, что эта горечь и боль ничего общего не имеет с чувством безнадежной угнетенности. Наоборот, впечатление от этой вещи, столь необычной по своей неприкрашенной и нелегкой правде, как бы освобождает душу от невысказанности того, что должно было быть высказано, и тем самым укрепляет в ней чувства мужественные и высокие.

Эта суровая повесть — еще один пример того, что нет таких участков или явлений действительности, которые были бы в наше время исключены из сферы советского художника и недоступны правдивому описанию. Все дело в том, какими возможностями располагает сам художник.

И еще один простой и поучительный вывод позволяет сделать эта повесть: истинно значительное содержание, верность большой жизненной правде, глубокая человечность в подходе к изображению даже самых трудных объектов не могут не призвать к жизни и соответствующей формы. В «Одном дне» она ярка и своеобразна в самой своей будничной обычности и внешней непритязательности, она менее всего озабочена самой собою и потому исполнена внутреннего достоинства и силы.

Я не хочу предвосхищать оценку читателями этого небольшого по объему произведения, хотя для меня несомненно, что оно означает приход в нашу литературу нового, своеобычного и вполне зрелого мастера.

Может быть, использование автором — весьма, впрочем, умеренное и целесообразное — некоторых словечек и речений той среды, где его герой проводит свой трудовой день, вызовет возражения особо привередливого вкуса. Но в целом «Один день Ивана Денисовича» — из ряда тех произведений литературы, восприняв которые мы испытываем большое желание, чтобы наше чувство признательности автору было разделено и другими читателями.

А. Твардовский.

В пять часов утра, как всегда, пробило подъем — молотком об рельс у штабного барака. Перерывистый звон слабо прошел сквозь стекла, намерзшие в два пальца, и скоро затих: холодно было, и надзирателю неохота была долго звонить.

Звон утих, а за окном все так же, как и среди ночи, когда Шухов вставал к параше, была тьма и тьма, да попадало в окно три желтых фонаря: два — на зоне, один — внутри лагеря.

И барака что-то не шли отпирать, и не слыхать было, чтобы дневальные брали бочку парашную на палки — выносить.

Шухов никогда не просыпал подъема, всегда вставал по нему — до развода было часа полтора времени своего, не казенного, и кто знает лагерную жизнь, всегда может подработать: шить кому-нибудь из старой подкладки чехол на рукавички; богатому бригаднику подать сухие валенки прямо на койку, чтоб ему босиком не топтаться вкруг кучи, не выбирать; или пробежать по каптеркам, где кому надо услужить, подмести или поднести что-нибудь; или идти в столовую собирать миски со столов и сносить их горками в посудомойку — тоже накормят, но там охотников много, отбою нет, а главное — если в миске что осталось, не удержишься, начнешь миски лизать. А Шухову крепко запомнились слова его первого бригадира Куземина — старый был лагерный волк, сидел к девятьсот сорок третьему году уже двенадцать лет и своему пополнению, привезенному с фронта, как-то на голой просеке у костра сказал:

— Здесь, ребята, закон — тайга. Но люди и здесь живут. В лагере вот кто погибает: кто миски лижет, кто на санчасть надеется да кто к куму ходит стучать.

Насчет кума — это, конечно, он загнул. Те-то себя сберегают. Только береженье их — на чужой крови.

Всегда Шухов по подъему вставал, а сегодня не встал. Еще с вечера ему было не по себе, не то знобило, не то ломало. И ночью не угрелся. Сквозь сон чудилось — то вроде совсем заболел, то отходил маленько. Все не хотелось, чтобы утро.

Но утро пришло своим чередом.

Да и где тут угреешься — на окне наледи наметано, и на стенах вдоль стыка с потолком по всему бараку — здоровый барак! — паутинка белая. Иней.

Шухов не вставал. Он лежал на верху вагонки, с головой накрывшись одеялом и бушлатом, а в телогрейку, в один подвернутый рукав, сунув обе ступни вместе. Он не видел, но по звукам все понимал, что делалось в бараке и в их бригадном углу. Вот, тяжело ступая по кори-

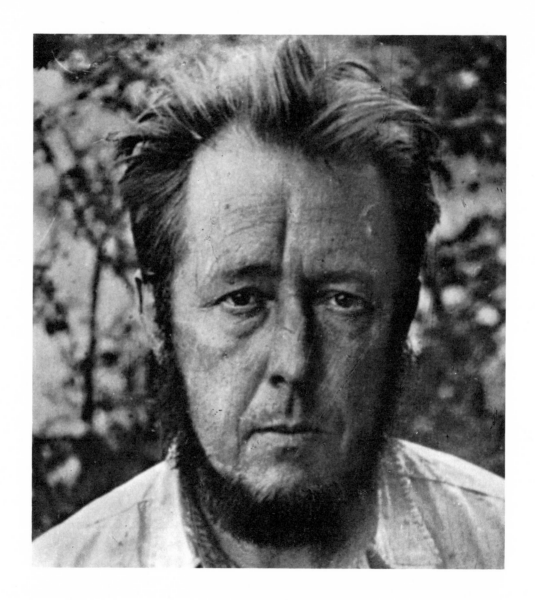

А. СОЛЖЕНИЦЫН

★

ЗАХАР-КАЛИТА́

Рассказ

Друзья мои, вы просите рассказать что-нибудь из летнего велосипедного? Ну вот, если нескучно, послушайте о Поле Куликовом.

Давно мы на него целились, но как-то всё дороги не ложились. Да ведь туда раскрашенные щиты не зазывают, указателей нет, и на карте найдешь не на каждой, хотя битва эта по четырнадцатому веку досталась русскому телу и русскому духу дороже, чем Бородино по девятнадцатому. Таких битв не на одних нас, а на всю Европу в полтысячи лет выпадала одна. Эта битва была не княжеств, не государственных армий — битва материков.

Может, мы и подбираться вздумали нескладно: от Епифани через Казановку и Монастырщину. Только потому, что дождей перед тем не было, мы проехали в седлах, за рули не тащили, а через Дон, еще не набравший глубины, и через Непрядву переводили свои «ве́лики» по пешеходным двудосочным мосткам.

Задолго, с высоты, мы увидели на другой обширной высоте как будто иглу в небо. Спустились — потеряли ее. Опять стали вытягивать вверх — и опять показалась серая игла, теперь уже явнее, а рядом с ней привиделась нам как будто церковь, но странная, постройки невиданной, какая только в сказке может примереститься: купола ее были как бы сквозные, прозрачные и в струях жаркого августовского дня колебались и морочили — то ли есть они, то ли нет.

Хорошо догадались мы в лощинке у колодца напиться и фляжки наполнить — это очень нам потом пригодилось. А мужичок, который ведро нам давал, на вопрос: «Где Поле Куликово?» — посмотрел на нас как на глупеньких:

— Да не Кулико́во, а Кули́ково. Подле поля-то деревня Кули́ковка, а Кулико́вка вона, на Дону, в другу сторону.

После этого мужичка мы пошли глухими проселками и до самого памятника несколько километров не встретили уже ни души. Просто это выпало нам так в тот день — ни души, в стороне где-то и помахивала тракторная жатка, и здесь тоже люди были не раз и придут не раз, потому что засеяно было все, сколько глаз охватывал, и доспевало уже — где греча, где свекла, клевер, овес и рожь, и горох (того гороху молодого и мы полущили),— а все же не было никого в тот день, и мы прошли как по священному безмолвному заповеднику. Нам без помех думалось о тех русоволосых ратниках, о девяти из каждого пришедшего десятка, которые вот тут, на сажень под теперешним наносом, легли и до́кости растворились в земле, чтоб только Русь встряхнулась от басурманов.

Throughout the years up to 1961, not only was I convinced that I would never in my life see a line of mine in print but I also did not dare read anything to most of even my close friends for fear of divulgence. Finally, when I was about forty-two, this secretiveness as a writer began to oppress me very much. The heaviest burden was the impossibility of having my work commented on by sophisticated literary readers. In 1961, following the Twenty-second Congress of the CPSU and Tvardovsky's speech at it, I decided to reveal myself and to offer "One Day in the Life of Ivan Denisovich."

Such self-revelation seemed to me then—not without good reason—very risky: it could lead to the destruction of all my manuscripts and of me myself. But at that point things turned out happily; after extended efforts, A. T. Tvardovsky succeeded in bringing out my novella a year later. But publication of my things was stopped almost immediately; my plays were held up, as was, in 1964, my novel "The First Circle," which in 1965 was confiscated, along with my archives from years back.

In those months it seemed to me that it was an unforgivable mistake to have exposed my work prematurely and that I would not be able to complete it.

We almost never can evaluate and, through consequences, immediately become fully conscious of events which have already happened to us; all the more unpredictable and surprising for us is the course of events to come.

A work of art contains its verification in itself: artificial, strained concepts do not withstand the test of being turned into images; they fall to pieces, turn out to be sickly and pale, convince no one. Works which draw on truth and present it to us in live and concentrated form grip us, compellingly involve us, and no one ever, not even ages hence, will come forth to refute them.

Nobel Lecture

А С

Мой дорогой
Доктор Хееб!

Дошли до меня слухи, будто на Западе неко-
торые любители сплетен или детективов распростра-
няют о Вас порочащие Вас домыслы: то будто вы
не являетесь истинным доверенным защитником моих
интересов, то будто даже действуете вопреки им.
Не удивительно, когда такие слухи возникали в самом
начале нашего с Вами сотрудничества — в конце 1969,
в начале 1970 года. Но то, что эти слухи возникают
и до сих пор — меня поражает нелепостью: как будто за два года я не имел бы возможности воз-
разить Вам публично в случае Вашей нелояльности
или некорректности.

Если эти слухи причиняют Вам досаду или кладут
пятно на Ваше доброе имя, — я искренно хотел бы,
дорогой доктор Хееб, как можно скорее и катего-
ричнее опровергнуть их публично, в любой форме,
какую Вы сочтете удобной. Я готов публично в самых сильных выражениях заявить, что я высочайше
ставлю Вашу честность и Ваши отличные деловые
качества и не мог бы сделать себе адвоката лучше
Вас.

Итак, если требуется подобное мое высказывание —
дайте мне рекомендацию, как и в какой форме
его сделать.

Разумеется, и само данное письмо Вы можете
рассматривать как подобный документ, сделать

его (и сам автограф) открытым, публичным, показывать кому угодно.

Несколько дней назад я просил Вас о лекарстве. Спешу сообщить, что необходимость в нем отпала, и если Вы еще не предпринимали ничего — то и не надо. Так же и Вiс'ов я пока достал немного, и срочности тоже нет.

Самые добрые пожелания Вашим близким!
С самым глубоким почтением, доверием
       и расположением
              Ваш

There are many ways to kill a poet.
For Tvardovsky they chose taking away his creation,
his passion—his magazine.
The sixteen years of humiliations meekly borne
by this noble knight were not enough.
If only the magazine held out; if only literary tradition
were not broken off; if only people were published;
if only people read.
Not enough; they added the fires of rout, havoc,
and injustice. The flames burned into him in six months.
Six months later he was mortally ill
and only because of habitual fortitude
lived until now, until his last hour,
fully conscious, suffering.

A Word for the Dead

Traveling along country roads in central Russia, you begin to understand why the Russian countryside has such a soothing effect.

It is because of its churches. They rise over ridge and hillside, descending toward wide rivers like red and white princesses, towering above the thatch and wooden huts of everyday life with their slender, carved and fretted belfries. From far away they greet each other; from distant, unseen villages they rise toward the same sky.

Wherever you may wander, over field or pasture, many miles from any homestead, you are never alone: above the wall of trees, above the hayricks, even above the very curve of the earth itself, the dome of a belfry is always beckoning to you, from Borki Lovetskie, Lyubichi, or Gavrilovskoe.

But as soon as you enter a village you realize that the churches which welcomed you from afar are no longer living.

A Journey along the Oka

How easy for me to live with You, O Lord!
How easy for me to believe in You!
When my mind parts in bewilderment
or falters,
when the most intelligent people see no further
than this day's end
and do not know what must be done tomorrow,
You grant me the serene certitude
that You exist and that You will take care
that not all the paths of good be closed.
Atop the ridge of earthly fame,
I look back in wonder at the path
which I alone could never have found,
a wondrous path through despair to this point
from which I, too, could transmit to mankind
a reflection of Your rays.
And as much as I must still reflect
You will give me.
But as much as I cannot take up
You will have already assigned to others.

notes

illustrations

with position finding. Solzhenitsyn was sent to the northwest front.

At the same time. Near Staraya Russa.

Near Novosil, May 1943. Transferred to the central front, near Orel, Solzhenitsyn met his old schoolmate Nicholas Vitkevich, assigned to a neighboring division. Solzhenitsyn's unit included a photography section, hence the possibility of these good negatives, hard to come by on the front lines. The meeting with Vitkevich was the beginning of the correspondence that brought both friends to prison. The photographs became part of the prosecution's evidence.

21 After the capture of Orel, August 1943. At the conclusion of this battle, Solzhenitsyn was decorated with the Order of the Patriotic War and promoted to first lieutenant.

February 1944. In a bombproof dugout at Shiparniya. For many months, the big offensive was followed by immobility in the trenches. Solzhenitsyn wrote stories about the war, sending them to a Moscow review, which refused them.

28 Summer 1946, Moscow. Kaluga Camp. There exists no photograph of Solzhenitsyn at the time of his arrest or during the earliest months he spent in prison. His first chance to be photographed came in this Moscow camp, which was charged with the job of constructing Building No. 30 along the present-day Leninsky Prospekt.

29 Workyard on the Leninsky Prospekt.

32 December 1948. In the Moscow sharashka. By way of compensation for his work, Solzhenitsyn received permission to be photographed. For this occasion he was lent a suit of civilian clothes.

Quite coincidentally, the picture was taken on December 11, his thirtieth birthday. He looks somewhat as Gleb Nerzhin of "The First Circle" would look, though this was a year earlier than the events described in the book.

33 Winter 1949-50, at the time of the events described in "The First Circle." This pencil portrait was made in several sittings by the painter Ivashev-Musatov (Kondrashev-Ivanov in the novel) in the common room of the Mavrino sharashka.

35 In the special camp, on the day Solzhenitsyn was released.

36 In Tashkent.

37 March 1953. In Kokterek, in Kazakhstan. Solzhenitsyn was free, but condemned to perpetual exile. This photograph was required by the employment agency and paid for out of Solzhenitsyn's last funds at the time of his release. The ex-prisoner is wearing the clothes he had on at the time of his arrest. His officer's pea jacket was still in good condition, since Solzhenitsyn had been forbidden to wear it during his camp years.

39 Tashkent, marketplace.

42 Kokterek.

44 Summer 1955. Two years have passed. Solzhenitsyn has earned enough money to buy a little house made of clay. At the window, on a summer day, as sunrise illuminates the steppe.

In his house, Solzhenitsyn sleeps on packing cases.

He has also been able to buy a camera, to reproduce the manuscripts that were beginning to accumulate: three plays, a poem ("Shosse Entuziastov"), and the early chapters of "The First Circle." With this same camera, Solzhenitsyn photographed himself at his writing table. He is wearing his finest shirt, bought in a large Tashkent store, which he later described in "Cancer Ward."

No one can predict the future, not the most powerful state any more than its humblest prisoners. In far-off Moscow, profound upheavals have taken place, and the exiles in Kazakhstan are released. During his three years' exile, Solzhenitsyn slept on packing cases: here, on the eve of his departure in 1956, he has the satisfaction of throwing them out.

texts

letter to Dr. Heeb

September 3, 1971

My dear Dr. Heeb:

Reports have reached me that in the West certain lovers of gossip or detective novels are spreading fantastic stories maligning you: supposedly you are not a duly authorized defender of my interests, you supposedly even act against them. It was not surprising when such rumors arose at the very beginning of our collaboration in late 1969, early 1970. But the fact that these rumors are to this day still cropping up astonishes me by its absurdity: supposedly for the last two years I would have had no opportunity of publicly reproving you in case of your disloyalty or tactlessness.

If these rumors cause you annoyance or blemish your good name, I would sincerely like, dear Dr. Heeb, as soon and as categorically as possible to deny them publicly in whatever form you consider appropriate. I am prepared publicly to state, in the strongest terms, that I have the highest opinion of your integrity and your excellent professional qualities and that I could not wish for a better attorney than you.

So, if such a statement by me is necessary, advise me how and in what form to put it.

Naturally, you may consider this very letter as just such a document and make it (and the autograph) known, public, available to anyone.

A few days ago I asked you for some medicine. I hasten to tell you that the need for it has disappeared, and that if you haven't done anything about it, please don't bother. And for the time being I've gotten a few Bics, too, so there's no urgency there.

My best wishes to your family!

With the deepest respect, confidence, and affectionate regards,